SPYING, SURVEILLANCE, AND
PRIVACY IN THE 21st CENTURY

When Companies
Spy on You
Corporate Data Mining and Big Business

Jeri Freedman

Cavendish
Square

New York

Published in 2018 by Cavendish Square Publishing, LLC
243 5th Avenue, Suite 136, New York, NY 10016

Library of Congress Cataloging-in-Publication Data

Names: Freedman, Jeri.
Title: When companies spy on you: corporate data mining and big business / Jeri Freedman.
Description: New York : Cavendish Square, 2018. | Series: Spying, surveillance, and privacy in the 21st-century | Includes index.
Identifiers: ISBN 9781502626752 (library bound) | ISBN 9781502626707 (ebook)
Subjects: LCSH: Data mining. | Business--Data processing.
Classification: LCC HF5415.125 F74 2018 | DDC 658.8'02--dc23

Editorial Director: David McNamara
Editor: Fletcher Doyle
Copy Editor: Nathan Heidelberger
Associate Art Director: Amy Greenan
Designer: Stephanie Flecha
Production Coordinator: Karol Szymczuk
Photo Research: J8 Media

Contents

Huge banks of computers capture and analyze data about people's lives, activities, and purchases.

Data Mining and Big Business

I n 1949, George Orwell wrote the book *Nineteen Eighty-Four*. One of the key elements of the book was the government's constant surveillance of people's activities. Today, our daily activities are under constant surveillance, but not by the government. Rather, corporations are monitoring our purchases, entertainment choices, travel plans, eating preferences, and almost every other element of our lives. Every time we make an online purchase, or even view an item online, that data is recorded. Corporations know our personal details and preferences. They use that information for a variety of purposes, some of them useful, some annoying. The vast collection and sharing of personal data has made it extremely difficult to keep any part of our lives and habits private.

At the heart of this situation is data mining. Data mining is the collection and analysis of large amounts of data in order to reveal **correlations** (relationships). An example of such a correlation is "people who buy canned chicken noodle soup also often purchase children's clothing." As can be seen from this example, one major purpose of data mining is to find ways to target people with appropriate marketing information to get them to buy things. In recent years, the process of data mining for commercial purposes has been refined to determine the items and services a specific person is likely to purchase. The desire of companies to profile their customers this way has fueled the efforts of companies to acquire as much information as possible about individuals, which can then be used for marketing purposes.

How Data Mining Works

Data consists of pieces of information that can be identified by, recorded on, and processed by a computer. Data includes facts (such as the items a person has purchased) and numbers (such as the cost of those items, or the buyer's age). Today, companies can acquire massive quantities of data because so many activities are carried out via computer, from **point-of-sale systems** in stores and restaurants, to online purchases, to forms that are either filled out online or completed manually and later entered into computer systems for storage. Other data comes from companies' internal systems, including their sales, inventory, payroll, and accounting systems.

This data can be used to provide information that will help companies enhance their profitability. However, in order to obtain useful information from this huge pool of data, it is necessary to identify patterns or relationships among the data. Information might include the products that sell to a certain age group, or the time of year when they sell, for example. Information, in turn, can generate knowledge. Knowledge includes elements such as past trends and predictions of likely future trends. For example, analysis of the customers' response to past **promotions** can shed light on consumers' buying habits. They may be more likely to respond to promotions for some types of items than for others.

As the reach and power of computer systems have grown, there have been great advances in companies' ability to capture, transmit, and process data. Large increases in computer storage capacity have allowed companies to **integrate** the **databases** from various departments to look for relationships in the data that is stored on different systems, such as sales, inventory, and accounting. The result has been the creation of **"data warehouses," consolidated** systems that store huge amounts of data from various systems. Data warehousing provides a means for companies to centrally access and manage their data. Advances in data analysis software have increased companies' ability to manage and analyze this data to identify relationships and trends. The value of this data is not lost on the corporations that collect it. Many companies have started selling data about their customers to other companies in related businesses or industries that can use it to identify and market to potential customers.

Among the most significant users of data mining are retail, financial, and communications companies—all types of companies focused on selling products to consumers, both individually and as groups. On an individual level, a company can analyze a customer's buying history and send the customer promotions, such as free shipping or coupons with discounts, for the specific types of items he or she buys. This process is called "targeted promotion." When the company sends a customer advertisements for the specific types of items he or she buys, this is called "targeted advertising." This is what happens when a retailer sends recommendations to specific customers based on their past purchases or items they have viewed.

Companies can also use data mining to analyze demographic data to target promotions to particular segments of consumers. Demographics are personal characteristics such as the age and gender of purchasers, or the geographic area in which they live.

Data Mining Is Everywhere

Data-mining applications are available for all sizes of businesses. Data-mining applications exist for giant integrated computer systems of large corporations and the **client/server systems** used by small businesses. They can be run on remote computer systems in the "**cloud,**" as well as on-site. They are available in all price ranges, from a few thousand dollars to over one million dollars, depending on their size and complexity. The nature of the data-mining applications used depends on the size of the database and the number and complexity of queries, or questions, being asked.

Data is analyzed by means of complex rules written in computer code. These coded instructions are called "**algorithms.**" These data-mining algorithms are very complicated and understood only by computer scientists. However, the people who use the data-mining applications do not have to apply the algorithms directly. Instead, they have a set of tools that allows them to query, or ask questions of, the database in an easily understandable and more **natural language.**

The massive amount of data accumulated by companies is called "big data," and it is everywhere today. Computer scientists and business managers are constantly trying to find new and improved ways to collect, analyze, and profit from data. At the same time, individuals and privacy advocates have become more and more concerned about the collection and use of people's personal data.

Really Big Data

Most **transactions** people engage in today leave a digital "footprint." The details of each transaction are captured and stored in a computer system. Every year the amount of data grows faster than the previous year. There are a number of reasons for this. Every year a greater number of commercial and entertainment transactions are being done online rather than in brick-and-mortar facilities. More stores and businesses are using computerized systems to process their in-store transactions as well. For example, many restaurants are having customers pay their bill and fill out surveys electronically at the table after a meal. More and more businesses are engaging in data capture and mining.

Why are companies so interested in capturing this data? According to Bernard Marr, a typical Fortune 1000 company can generate more than $65 million from just a 10 percent increase in data. Retailers can increase their profits by using data mining. In 2014, 73 percent of companies surveyed by

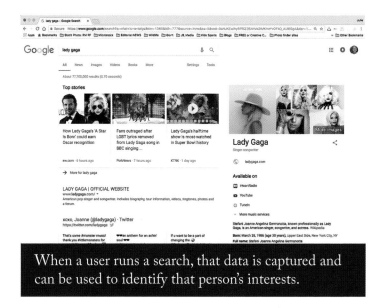

When a user runs a search, that data is captured and can be used to identify that person's interests.

the research firm Gartner had already invested in big data or planned to do so by 2016. There is tremendous potential for companies in data mining, given that as of 2015 only 0.5 percent of all the data collected was analyzed. Far more data is collected than can be digested. The enormous amount of this data makes it impossible for people to process it without automated tools. Data mining automates the process of analyzing this data.

Where does all this data come from? Some comes from online transactions on retail, financial, and other commercial websites. Some comes from online searches. Every second, forty thousand searches are run just on Google. Other data comes from social media. More than one billion people use Facebook every day. Twitter has more than three hundred million users who transmit more than five hundred million tweets per day. Approximately three hundred hours of video are uploaded to YouTube per minute. In 2015, about one trillion photos were shared online, about 80 percent of which were taken on smartphones. The same year, more than 1.4 billion smartphones were shipped. By 2020, more than thirty billion smart devices will be connected worldwide, or approximately four devices for every person.

Discovering Connections

Information extracted from data is used for two purposes: description and prediction. Data mining processes the data to find relationships and patterns and presents them in a simplified format that can be easily understood. Specific applications for data-mining methods are tailored for particular needs and goals. However, there are several general types of pattern detection that are commonly used, and these can provide some insight into how data mining works.

Anomaly detection: In this case, the data is analyzed to find the data that doesn't fit into a typical pattern. Take, for example, a paper a student has written. The teacher has a number of pieces of data in the form of past assignments written by the student. These contain certain phrasings, grammatical errors, and a recognizable vocabulary level. When the student turns in a paper that is radically different in quality from his or her preceding work, the teacher flags it as an **anomaly**—something that doesn't fit into the pattern of the other data—and suspects that it is copied from another source. Data-mining applications do the same sort of thing, but they process much larger quantities of data faster. They can, for example, identify an income tax return or invoice as **atypical** and flag it for review.

Association learning: This type of application attempts to match similar types of items. It is the basis for online

They Know Everything About You

Facebook tracks users' behavior to select which ads to show them. Objections from users have caused the company to give users the option to opt out of data collection. However, if users don't exercise this option, the company knows everything they do on the site. A 2013 study from Cambridge University in the United Kingdom revealed that, from users' "likes," researchers can make a reasonable guess about their characteristics—such as whether they lean to the right or left politically, their sexual preference, religion, intelligence,

Data captured by social media applications can identify people's personal characteristics, such as political leaning.

and substance abuse. Target's mailer tracker system tracks the purchases of customers, and then mails them coupons for other products that might interest them. The practice became seriously disturbing for one customer when, according to a CNN report, "the mailer system analyzed her previous purchases and noticed that what she was buying in terms of groceries and toiletries fit a trend that usually meant a customer was in the early stages of pregnancy. Unfortunately, the girl and her family didn't know that yet. Sure enough, though, the mailer system was right, the girl was pregnant."

These are just a few of the means that companies are using to gather information about customers. Targeting their ads at customers isn't all they do with that information. Many companies sell customer information to other companies, which in turn target their own marketing material at them. So there is no telling where your information might end up.

shopping applications that recommend items that are similar to ones customers have previously bought. Did you buy the latest Star Wars book? You are likely to get recommendations for books of a similar sort when you log in. The same thing happens when you watch movies on Netflix.

Cluster detection: A computer algorithm can separate people into different groups according to shared characteristics. For example, people who frequent websites of nurseries or buy a number of gardening tools are likely to be gardeners, and hence might be interested in a variety of products related to gardening.

Classification: In classification, a computer algorithm is given a set of rules, which it can apply to differentiate various types of data. This is the approach used to distinguish spam from legitimate emails.

Regression: Regression is a statistical method that can be automated for data mining. In regression, past usage patterns are studied in order to predict what a person is likely to do in the future. This approach can be used for applications that predict what types of activities a person might engage in, in the future, such as traveling for pleasure. It can also be used by media companies to identify the types of apps or features that will increase the use of their site or viewing of their video presentations.

The purpose of all these approaches is to use the power of data mining to find ways to engage users and customers to a greater degree.

The History of Marketing

The biggest driver of data mining and the collection of information is sales and marketing. Ever since people

This handbill is typical of those given out or posted to advertise products in the nineteenth century.

Data Insecurity

On December 14, 2016, Yahoo! revealed that in 2013 it was hacked, and data from one billion users was stolen. The revelation followed an admission made in September 2016 that the data of about five hundred million users had been stolen in 2014, as the result of a data breach. Prior to the announcement of this new breach, the 2014 hack was thought to be the largest cyber-based data theft ever. The data stolen included names, addresses, dates of birth, passwords, and encrypted and unencrypted security questions.

The Yahoo! data breaches illustrate several important factors about the collection and storage of people's data. First, the mere existence of large repositories of data about people makes them attractive targets for hackers. Information such as social security and credit card numbers, along with other personal information, is extremely valuable to criminals engaged in identity theft. Thus, the collection of individuals' data makes those people vulnerable to identity theft. There is a hot market among criminals for stolen credit card numbers with their expiration dates and security codes.

Other types of information about individuals make them vulnerable to other types of problems. For example, foreign governments have an interest in obtaining negative information about people who are in the government or running for office. A foreign government might use such information to embarrass a candidate. Because many people tend to use the same usernames and passwords for multiple accounts, breaches such as those at Yahoo! may leave people open to theft of money or other funds, such as IRS refunds.

In the case of the Yahoo! breach, the company stated that the same entity was believed to be involved in both breaches and that it was a state-sponsored effort. In other words, the hackers were acting on behalf of a government. In March 2017, after an investigation, the FBI charged two Russian intelligence officers in the 2014 hack. However, the earlier, larger hack remained under investigation.

Luckily, the Yahoo! hack did not include credit card or bank account numbers. The same is not true of other organizations that have been hacked, such as Target. In 2016, companies that experienced data breaches included restaurants, information technology services companies, health-care providers, universities, and the Internal Revenue Service. The prevalence of cyber-security breaches means that the companies that collect large amounts of data about individuals are not the only ones who know all about their customers; ill-intentioned strangers have access to a wide range of their personal information as well.

have had something to sell, they have been advertising and marketing their products and services. In the Corning Museum of Glass, in Corning, New York, is a piece of ancient **Sumerian** glassware (circa 3000 BCE) dating to not long after the discovery of how to make glass. When researchers translated the text engraved on the bottom, it said, "Buy all

Advertisers have always embraced new media, as illustrated by this 1951 Pepsi television ad.

glass at Ahkmed's." Craftsmen—and later, companies—have long struggled to identify and attract customers. For most of human history, advertising took a **scattershot** approach. Prior to the twentieth century, most advertising appeared in magazines, newspapers, handbills given to passersby, or posters placed prominently on buildings.

The advent of electrical technology at the end of the nineteenth century laid the groundwork for radically new types of advertising in the twentieth century. One of the first of these new technologies, beginning in the 1920s, was the radio, which allowed sponsors of programs to pitch their products directly to listeners, as if they were speaking to them in person. Television, developed in the 1940s, became a household staple by the 1950s. Television allowed advertisers to show as well as talk about their products, ushering in the **heyday** of mass marketing. All these technologies had one thing in common: they were aimed at the public at large, or at very large segments of the public such as housewives or children. Companies hoped that the advertisement would be seen by people who wanted or needed the product. However, beyond targeting probable viewers or listeners—there were a lot of advertisements for beer and razor blades during baseball broadcasts, for example—there was no attempt to identify in advance exactly who those people were. As advertising became more expensive and competition grew, there was clearly a need to identify which members of the pubic were actually likely to buy a product.

Beginning in the 1960s, companies began to seek ways to segment their potential customer base. This process mostly took the form of using surveys to identify existing customers. That information could be used to target advertising mailings and TV ads to that segment of the market. This concept is

Facebook and other companies are developing
artificial intelligence processes that will allow
computers to draw their own conclusions from data.

still the basis of data mining. Companies in a given industry are often competing with other companies for the same customers. The only way to increase sales is to take customers from competitors or to find new potential customers who can be targeted. Marketing only to customers likely to buy the product can significantly reduce marketing expenses. In the late twentieth and twenty-first centuries, technology has continued to evolve. The internet allowed the creation of click-through ads. In this case, customers who were interested could click on an ad. Instead of having to search for potential customers, companies could let them use this "inbound" marketing to select themselves. The next logical step was to use information about buyers to target ads to them—with a high probability that these ads would interest them.

The Evolution of Data Mining

The evolution of advertising has taken place hand in hand with the development of computer technology. The term "data mining" was coined in the 1990s, and "big data" even more recently. However, the technology behind data mining developed over a much longer time. The term "data science" is used by computer scientists and **statisticians** to describe the combination of statistics with computer technology, resulting in data mining, among other applications. In 1962, statistician John W. Tukey wrote a paper titled "The Future of Data Analysis," in which he defined "data analysis" as a form of statistics that could be used to establish which pieces of data are important. In his 1977 book, *Exploratory Data Analysis,* Tukey argues that data analysis should be approached from a scientific perspective. For example, a **hypothesis** (best guess as to what will be found) should be formulated, and then the data should be analyzed to see whether it supports or disproves the hypothesis. His ideas promoted the idea of data as a means of revealing information.

In 1977, the Information Sciences Institute (ISI) established a new division, the International Association for Statistical Computing (IASC). Its mission is to link "traditional statistical methodology, modern computer technology, and the knowledge of **domain experts** [experts in a particular subject] in order to convert data into information and knowledge." Data scientist Gregory Piatetsky-Shapiro organized the first Knowledge Discovery in Databases workshop in 1989. In 1995, it became an annual conference.

Data mining made the big time in September 1994, when *Business Week* published a cover story titled "Database Marketing." It described how companies were collecting mountains of data about individuals, crunching it to predict how likely they were to buy a product, and then using that knowledge to create precisely calibrated marketing messages. The article compared the new technology to the earlier use of barcode scanners to collect information. According to the article, "Many companies were too overwhelmed by the sheer quantity of data to do anything useful with the information … Still, many companies believe they have no choice but to brave the database-marketing frontier."

In 1996, Usama Fayyad, Gregory Piatetsky-Shapiro, and Padhraic Smyth published the article "From Data Mining to Knowledge Discovery in Databases" in *AI Magazine*. They defined "data mining" as a step in knowledge discovery from databases, a step consisting of "the application of specific algorithms for extracting patterns from data," whereas data preparation, data selection, data cleaning, incorporation of appropriate prior knowledge, and proper interpretation of the results of mining were defined as additional steps in the knowledge-discovery process. A year later, University of Michigan professor C. F. Jeff Wu, in his inaugural lecture for the H. C. Carver Chair of Statistics, called for statistics to be renamed "data science" and statisticians to be called "data scientists." That same year, the *Data Mining and Knowledge Discovery* journal was published for the first time. The use of "data mining" in its title illustrates how the term was eclipsing "knowledge discovery" to describe the process of analyzing large databases to acquire information.

In May 2005, Thomas H. Davenport, Don Cohen, and Al Jacobson of Babson College published a Babson Research Report, "Competing on Analytics." It described how companies were applying statistical analysis to data and using predictive modeling to achieve a competitive advantage.

Since then, data mining has become a mainstream organizational tool. Aside from business applications, it is used in science, engineering, medicine, finance, national security, and other areas to find relationships among data that are not otherwise readily identifiable. The widespread collection and use of big data is bringing down the cost of the technology, which in turn leads to even greater use. In addition, new devices capable of collecting and transmitting data are continuing to be developed. These two factors are likely to increase the collection and application of individuals' personal data.

The development of new data analysis tools hasn't stopped. Data scientists are exploring "deep learning" techniques. The focus of deep learning is to use a combination of data mining, data science, and **artificial intelligence** to identify relationships and patterns too complex to be identified with other data-mining techniques.

The Value of Data

Data has immense financial value both to the company that collects it and to other companies that might buy it. We live in a country where more than 70 percent of the economy consists of the purchases of goods and services by consumers. There is a finite number of consumers (although that number is large), and they have a finite amount of money (except for a small number of the super-rich). Therefore, the competition for those consumers is intense. Identifying which consumers are likely to use a company's products or services is critically important to companies, but merely identifying them is not enough. Consumers must be aware that the company's product or service exists, and they must be convinced that they need it. Therefore, the ability to target ads to individuals who are inclined to be interested can enhance a company's income and profit. In addition, companies that do not even sell a product or service, such as search engines and social media companies, have created revenue streams for themselves by selling the customer data itself.

Because data is valuable, companies have gone to great lengths to create and use digital tools to collect enormous amounts of data and analyze it. There are some socially beneficial applications of data mining. For instance, the collection and analysis of data on a large number of people with a particular disease might make it possible to identify which approaches to treatment work best for people with a particular cluster of characteristics. However, the constant collection of data on people every time they use a digital device, website, or app makes it very difficult for them to maintain any privacy. As time goes on, the collection of individuals' data is likely to become even more pervasive. New types of increasingly sophisticated tools, including those that rely on artificial intelligence, will be developed. All this will make it ever harder to keep any aspect of one's life and activities private.

A point-of-sale computer captures information about customers' purchases and food preferences.

# of Data Mining

U nquestionably, businesses have embraced data mining. The reason that data mining is so popular among businesses is that it works. It gives them the ability to find relationships that would be difficult, if not impossible, to identify by manual means. These relationships can then be leveraged to increase sales or streamline marketing, allowing companies to be more efficient, which lowers their costs. The fact is that data mining has important benefits for many types of organizations and some advantages for consumers as well.

Data mining is a part of a process called knowledge discovery. The goal of knowledge discovery is to find hidden information. The larger the set of data, the easier it is to discover meaningful relationships, and the more accurate the results will be. Data mining has been applied effectively in a number of fields, including business, weather forecasting, health care, manufacturing, transportation, finance, and insurance, among others. Companies have a variety of different systems filled with customer data: point-of-sale systems, websites, order tracking, accounts payable, and others. Using the data in these systems allows companies to provide a better experience for their customers. Providing an improved experience allows companies to make more money both overall and per customer. It also allows businesses to streamline their operations to minimize waste and make better use of their resources.

Advantages of Data-Mining Techniques for Companies

Data mining provides the means for companies to improve their revenues, efficiency, and profitability in a number of ways.

- *Data mining is useful for predicting future trends:* As people's behavior changes, or as new groups such as **millennials** emerge, these changes are revealed by data mining. The ability to spot trends early allows companies to adapt to them. Companies can change their product mix, add new features to products, or provide the ability to buy products on new devices.

- *Data mining reveals people's habits and behavior:* Companies can use this information to tailor their products, marketing, and online presence to their users' tastes, to keep them engaged. Further, people's habits often change over time—from watching TV, to watching DVDs, to streaming video on TV sets, to streaming video to tablets and smartphones, for example. Change happens at an ever-increasing pace, and data mining allows companies to keep track of changes in customers' behavior and adjust their offerings accordingly.

- *Data mining helps managers with decision making:* Today, there is a vast quantity of data from a wide range of departments in businesses. Data mining identifies key factors by analyzing the data in production, sales, finance, research and development, human resources, and other databases. This process allows managers to become better informed about factors that affect their business. It also reveals potential problems that might otherwise be overlooked.

- *Data mining can increase a company's revenues and profitability:* Data mining can provide information about products' profitability and problems. It can reveal which products are preferred to others, allowing a company to adjust its product mix and pricing structure, improve customer satisfaction and **retention**, and plan production more efficiently. It can also shed light on why certain products don't appeal to customers.

- *Data mining aids in fraud detection:* Because of its ability to analyze behavior, data mining can identify behaviors that are typical of fraudulent activity. The more quickly fraud is detected, the less money it costs the company.

Data mining is used for specific purposes in a number of industries, which are discussed here.

Retail

The retail industry consists of businesses that sell goods and services. Retail companies must find customers for their products and then get information to those customers so that they know what the company has to offer and why it would benefit them. To accomplish these goals, companies use advertising and marketing. Advertising tells customers about a product or service. Marketing includes email, snail mail, and telemarketing outreach to potential customers. It also includes promotions such as offering discounts, gifts, or newsletters to customers. Both advertising and marketing are expensive. Therefore, companies benefit from techniques that allow them to better target advertising and marketing to customers who are likely to have an interest in the product or service, instead of just doing mass mailings or paying for ads that are seen by an inappropriate audience.

Data mining provides the means for companies to use historical data to create a model of customers who are likely to respond to new marketing campaigns or promotions. These models can be applied to both physical and online marketing. Data mining also provides a method to identify new customers by using a variation of a technique called market-basket analysis. The basis of this approach is that customers who buy one product also buy other products. However, which products are often bought together may not be apparent. For example, Family Dollar used market-basket analysis to find out which types of products were most beneficial to promote in their sale circulars. They compared the effects of featuring underwear and laundry products. They found that, although sales of all featured items went up by about the same amount, featuring laundry products resulted in more sales of additional products. Both retailers and companies that provide marketing services to businesses are interested in using data mining to establish which products certain groups of customers are likely to buy together.

In addition, retailers can use this information to offer special promotions, such as a bundle of items or a discount to targeted customers. Often data mining uncovers unexpected shopping patterns, which can benefit retailers. In this way, data mining helps a retailer to discover new customer groups. Instead of using the same ad or marketing campaign for all customers, the retailer can then target different versions of its ad to different groups of customers, or the company might offer a different bundle of products to different groups of customers. For example, if it were established that millennials tend to buy "skinny bundles" of TV channels from cable providers but want the ability to watch TV on every electronic device they own, whereas retired males want 172 sports channels, the cable or satellite TV provider could target different offers to these different groups. Before data mining, companies could target customers from different demographics, but data mining allows customers to be broken down into more specific groups. For example, companies could guess that people with Hispanic last names might be interested in Spanish channels, but data mining might reveal that only Hispanic people living in certain areas are likely to actually be Spanish speakers. Data mining might also show that consumers may be more likely to be influenced on the basis of demographic characteristics unrelated to their ethnicity, such as their age, gender, or level of education.

Companies that use email as part of their marketing program can use data mining to ensure that the content of their email is relevant to the customer receiving it. This increases the chance that the recipient will read it, instead of deleting it. It also builds a better relationship with customers because it gives them the impression the company is willing to take the time to learn about their interests rather than just bombarding them with irrelevant information. Some companies go as far as making an email profile of each customer. They do this by setting up an ID for each customer, noting how often the customer opens email from the company, and tracking the information that successfully got the customer to look at the email. They can also note if the customer made a purchase as a result of the email. Using the information they learn, they can tailor emails to the customer's interests and increase the chance that the customer will respond positively to the email.

Retailers, as well as other types of businesses, can use data mining to optimize their website. Retailers can track what users look at on the website and identify which parts of the site attract customers and on which links they click. If customers are not responding to certain parts of the site, or are looking at items but not purchasing them, the online presentation can be adjusted to improve users' responses, or incentives can be added to encourage a purchase. Because many companies have a very large volume of consumers viewing their site, data mining is required to analyze the behavior of this pool of users in a meaningful way.

Data mining can help a business improve its profitability, not just by increasing sales but also by measuring which advertising and marketing campaigns work. It can analyze customers' responses to these campaigns, allowing the company to use its resources more effectively and waste less money. Companies can also use data mining to identify which customers are likely to buy a product without an incentive, and which customers will probably require a special offer or discount to initiate a purchase. Thus, companies can target incentives to particular groups of customers, rather than to all customers, which again saves the company money.

Data mining plays a key role in customer relationship management (CRM). The goal of CRM is to retain customers and obtain repeat business. Because data mining provides insight into what is important to customers, the company can better understand their needs. By offering them products and services that meet their requirements, a company is more likely to retain customers. In addition, by observing what customers like and dislike about products, companies can modify their offerings to better appeal to them. Data mining can be used by service companies as well as by those selling goods. Often prices for services vary little from company to company because of competition. For instance, phone, internet, cable and satellite TV, and other types of providers often offer products that are similarly priced. What differentiates one company from another is the quality of their service and delivery to customers. Service companies can use data mining to see what services a given customer uses most and offer him or her custom packages. The company can also concentrate on enhancing those aspects of its service that customers value most or improving those that customers are not satisfied with. For example, a mobile provider might offer customers more data usage for a flat fee during the hours when they use their device the most.

Some customers are more valuable to a company than others. A small percentage of customers may represent the majority of a company's income. For a company with a large number of customers, data mining can be used to identify who

Human resources pros use data analytics to identify desirable characteristics in potential employees.

the most valuable customers are. Data mining can help the company identify the products, features, and other aspects of the customer relationship that the most valuable customers care about most. The more a company knows about its key customers, the better it can anticipate their needs and the better the service it can provide.

Employee Screening

Data mining also is used by human resources (HR) departments to identify the characteristics of successful employees. These characteristics may not always be obvious. For example, data mining might reveal that, in a technology company, the most successful salespeople are often English or liberal arts majors, not engineers. Their ability to understand and communicate with potential customers has more effect than a deep technical understanding of what makes the product tick. Thus, when hiring salespeople, HR may want to focus more on applicants with those skills and less on technical knowledge.

Finance

Both banking and stock trading rely heavily on data. Professionals in both industries are always looking for ways to improve their data-based decision making. Banks use data mining to build models based on historical customer data. The models help banks figure out which customers seeking loans are likely to be good credit risks. They also use data mining to establish customers' purchase patterns and to flag anomalous transactions that may be fraudulent. The bank can check with the customer to see if the transaction is legitimate. This saves the bank or credit card company—and the customer—a great deal of aggravation. It reduces the

Fast Fact

According to the research firm Gartner, more than 75 percent of organizations surveyed in 2015 had already invested in or planned to invest soon in big data. The International Data Corporation forecasts that big data revenue will climb "from $130.1 billion in 2016 to more than $203 billion in 2020."

Investment professionals use data analysis to find the best stocks to buy and sell at a given time.

bank's losses since it is responsible for covering most of the cost of fraudulent transactions on credit cards, and it helps protect the consumer from the activities of people committing fraud. Stock traders use data mining to uncover patterns of trading in specific stocks, sectors of the market such as energy, or the market as a whole. They use these patterns to guide their own investment decisions.

Every new technology provides yet another avenue for data mining. A recent trend is text mining. Text mining digitally culls the content of articles in newspapers and magazines. Firms use software to analyze the natural language in these articles, using text as if it were data.

Investment firms, for example, use computer programs to automatically mine the text of articles for keywords and use this information to make buy and sell decisions. Text mining is often used in combination with traditional data mining. This combination is called "text and data mining," or TDM. TDM relies on advanced software that breaks down digital information into numeric data and text, analyzes it, and produces a list of relationships. TDM can be applied to a variety of fields, but one major area where it is used is stock trading. Wall Street investment firms buy a license from a news source such as Associated Press, which allows them to monitor news feeds. The traders then apply TDM to the news stream to mine it for clues to predict which way stocks are likely to go. Associated Press licenses "machine-readable news products" to its customers, which can be streamed directly to computers that analyze them.

There is no question that TDM is bringing new streams of revenue to companies that publish news, such as Associated Press and Reuters. Whether it turns out to be of great utility to traders remains to be seen. The news feeds often provide only a brief summary of a company's financial results or the activities of a government agency, for example. Firms engaging in automated trading, determined to move before their competition, often end up making trading decisions based on this superficial and incomplete data, which could be misleading.

TDM could be used with scientific journals to weed through large quantities of data to throw light on hidden relationships that could lead to important breakthroughs in fields such as medicine. A growing number of publishers are looking for ways to capitalize on text mining. Media

In 2015, more than 1.4 billion smartphones were shipped. These phones contain sensors that can collect a variety of data. Applications on the phones collect user-entered data as well.

companies and public relations firms are also exploring ways to use text mining in their fields.

Manufacturing

Manufacturers, like retailers, must move with the times. Manufacturing companies today must capture and analyze large amounts of data from automated systems in order to operate efficiently and ensure the quality of their products. They can use data mining to analyze production data, to detect defective products and equipment, and to optimize settings for equipment. It can also be used to identify conditions or variations in processes at different plants that lead to defects.

In addition, data mining allows manufacturing plants to more accurately forecast how much product they need to produce and the amount of material and parts they will need. Better operations planning allows them to reduce inventory and control costs. Further, they can use data mining to analyze their supply chain and improve their ordering processes to minimize problems such as having too much or too little inventory. Like retail outlets, manufacturing

In an automated warehouse, robots locate and deliver items, and provide data to adjust inventory levels.

facilities have customers, even if these are other businesses rather than consumers. Therefore, many of the same types of advantages that retailers get from data mining are realized by manufacturers.

Benefits of Data Mining for Consumers

Consumers also see some benefits from the collection and analysis of data by companies. The following sections discuss these benefits in specific industries.

When a customer makes an online purchase, the company records the data to learn what people buy.

Retail

Having more accurate information about what consumers want helps companies provide products that incorporate features they prefer. In the past, companies have relied on consumers to fill out surveys to measure their satisfaction and preferences. This is still done today, but there are problems with surveys. For instance, what consumers say they want or like is often not what they purchase in reality. For example, they may say "variety" is the most important factor in choosing a store at which to shop, but actually they may go to a store that offers less variety but also charges less. In addition, many people don't fill out the surveys. Therefore, the responses may not represent a cross section of people, or they may not represent the most desirable customers—those who have the most money but are too busy to fill out endless surveys.

Data mining uses data that reflects actual customer purchases and behavior, so the information received by companies reveals what customers really do and want. It also provides the opinions of a large pool of customers across all demographics, not just those of a self-selected subset of customers. Data mining customers' information helps companies provide products and features that customers really want. The same is true with the qualities of products such as sizes, colors, or materials. Data mining can encourage retailers to provide consumers with discounts on items they want most because the company knows it will sell enough of them to make up for earning less on each unit sold. Data mining of consumer purchases can also be used in the reverse way. If companies find that certain products appeal less to consumers, they can be offered at steep discounts.

Customers often need help when deciding which product to buy, and they frequently have difficulty finding the information they need. Data mining provides companies with information about their customers, which they can use to provide information and answers to frequently asked questions (FAQs). They can mine their customer service databases for questions that customers frequently ask about their products and significantly improve the descriptive information they provide in their online and catalog entries so that people have the information they need. Companies can also add that information to the FAQ section of their websites. Often the FAQs contain only information the company assumes the customers need, such as how to return a product or change their address. However, these sections may lack information that many customers want, such as how long it will be before a back-ordered product is available, or even how to find this information—questions that didn't occur to the developer creating the FAQs. Using data mining to identify which questions appear repeatedly in the customer service database could result in better information being available to customers, as well as a reduction in customer service calls.

Data mining also allows retailers to anticipate the needs of customers. For example, if a customer has purchased a cluster of items that indicates that he or she has children, the site can show versions of products that are childproof at the top of the listing when the customer does a search, helping the customer find what he or she needs without searching through a long list of items.

As consumers' tastes and behaviors change, data mining information reflects these trends. Therefore, companies can react more rapidly to change their offerings to keep giving customers what they want. In this way, a symbiotic relationship is created between customers and retailers. As customers use features such as "recommendations," and find them valuable, this increases their trust in the retailer and their willingness to share additional information about themselves. In turn, the company can use the information to provide even more accurate suggestions to the customer. The goal of the company is to establish what the users want to see and provide it to them with as little effort on the part of customers as possible. This is especially important when dealing with customers who are accessing a retailer's website via a mobile device. Users of mobile devices need to interact with as few clicks as possible.

Therefore, the better the company can predict what the user wants to see, and the easier it makes selecting the right item, the more likely customers are to buy things from that site with their mobile devices. The less aggravating the process of locating and purchasing an item is for the customers, the more likely they are to make a purchase.

Data mining provides insight into which products customers tend to buy together. This information can be used by stores to locate these products in close proximity to each other, in both brick-and-mortar and online stores. This not only helps retailers sell more products but also makes it more convenient for customers to find what they're looking for without having to go to different locations.

In addition to helping companies provide better products and services, and keep up with changing tastes, data mining eliminates the need for customers to constantly fill out surveys, since the data is collected automatically. All of these applications of data mining increase customers' satisfaction with the purchasing process and improve the likelihood they will find a product satisfactory when they receive it, reducing the chances that they will have to go through the annoying process of repackaging it and returning it.

Personal Finance

One area where the sharing of consumers' information might help people is personal finance. The federal Task Force on Smart Disclosure aims to protect consumers applying for loans by making sure they have an understanding of all the terms, fees, and interest associated with the loans being proposed to them. In 2012, President Barack Obama charged the task force with collecting and organizing consumer information in a manner that assists consumers in making good financial decisions. The concept behind the plan is that a better understanding of how consumers spend would help them address problem areas. It would also give banks a better understanding of their customers. Given that most people have a poor understanding of personal finance, also known as financial literacy, the idea is to better educate them. If people understand their finances, they will make better decisions about taking out loans and mortgages, and this in turn will help prevent another financial meltdown like the one in 2008, which was caused by banks taking on too many mortgages from people who were bad credit risks.

One difficulty is how to perform the collection and analysis of information while still respecting people's privacy. In a 2012 *Time* magazine article, Chris Vein, a White House staff member for technology innovation, provided an example of how the process was used in one case. Government officials arranged for three water utilities in California to collect and provide statistics to customers on their water usage. One family found that they were using enormous amounts of water compared to their neighbors. Upon investigation, the family found their daughter was taking hour-long showers. When they made her shorten the length of her showers, their water bill dropped dramatically.

The idea is to apply this method to other areas affecting people's finances. For instance, banks and credit card companies can provide a breakdown of what people are spending their money on in order to give them better control over their finances as well as insight into who is profligate and who has better control. However, the task force would like to go further, capturing data from third parties and using that data to create a model of where people spend.

The task force would then generate guidelines and apps for consumers. An example of such an app would be a tool that allows consumers to compare the real cost of different types of mortgages while they are talking to a lender. Apps could even be created that compare terms and fees for the same product, similar to the way that the app from travel company Trivago allows customers to compare hotels. However, banks, mortgage brokers, and **payday lenders** (lenders who give short-term loans to tide people over between paychecks) are reluctant to share their information. They claim that their reluctance stems from a desire to keep their information out of the hands of competitors, but in reality transparent pricing would reduce the money they make from fees, charges, and hidden interest-rate increases.

Health Care

Today, medicine is often practiced in a trial-and-error fashion, as it has been for centuries. Physicians visually and verbally collect information about a patient's symptoms and family history, and possibly order blood tests or scans. They then make a best guess as to what the patient's problem is and consider the medications or treatments they're familiar with for treating it. They prescribe the medication or treatment, see if it works, and if not, they try another one.

Some types of treatments, especially for diseases such as cancer, work better on some people than others. In many cases, the faster effective treatment is applied, the better the chance of successfully treating the disease. If there were a better way to identify which treatment(s) would be most likely to be effective for a given patient, his or her chances of survival could be increased. In addition, some diseases are rare and therefore hard to diagnose. Often

Data Mining for Social Causes

Data mining has applications in social service as well as business. DoSomething.org is an organization that mobilizes young people to engage in positive causes. It is supported by more than a dozen major companies, including Johnson and Johnson, CVS, Coca-Cola, and Google. One of the subsidiaries of DoSomething.org is Crisis Text Line (CTL), which uses text messaging to provide anonymous chat services to teens in crisis. It provides support for teens dealing with problems such as depression, bullying, and sexual abuse. Teens text CTL and a trained professional engages them in an anonymous conversation. The conversations are saved digitally, along with the time of the conversation and geographic locations. Researchers are data mining from the more than 3.3 million text messages the crisis line has received to look for patterns that could be used to prevent or better address these problems. Among the organizations exploring the data are Johns Hopkins University, the Massachusetts Institute of Technology, and the University of Rochester. Other institutions—such as the University of California at Berkeley, Princeton, and Stanford—are considering doing so as well. Because the communications are anonymous, no personal information is compromised.

The data can be used by other types of organizations as well, including schools, government agencies, and others that want to help teens by preventing these problems from reaching the crisis stage. Knowing when and where problems repeatedly occur allows investigative and preventative actions to be taken. For example, researchers have found that teens

Data collected by crisis-intervention organizations can be used to better help troubled young people.

are more inclined to feel depressed at certain times of the day. Another example is identifying that students at a particular school are calling in about bullying at a specific time of day, which indicates that there is a problem that needs to be addressed. Other organizations such as human rights groups could use data mining in a similar way to identify patterns of abuse among their constituencies.

Analysis of patients' data allows doctors to make a more accurate diagnosis when a person becomes ill.

the symptoms are mistaken for those of another disease, or no diagnosis is made. If it were possible to compare the patient's demographic and genetic information with that of other people who have had the same symptoms, the results might reveal the true cause.

Massive amounts of data exist in medical databases in hospitals and other medical facilities, including information on the course and treatment of illnesses, as well as genetic information. This data could provide insight into who is most likely to experience a particular disease and what types of treatment are likely to be effective for people with a given cluster of demographic, genetic, or environmental factors. Using data mining to create **knowledge bases** of information that could be accessed remotely by physicians could significantly improve the diagnosis and treatment of disease, extending and saving lives. Such information can also be used to create standards for treatment that are based on hard data rather than on the anecdotal experience of doctors.

As mentioned previously, data mining has been used in many industries to create predictive models. It could be used in the same way in health care to predict the outcomes of treatments. Data mining could be used to create programs to identify patients at high risk for specific diseases and to intervene sooner. Such programs could reduce the number of treatments and hospital visits required, reducing the cost for the patient. Better treatment sooner could reduce patients' suffering and improve their chances of survival. Rapid, correct identification of patients' nonfatal illnesses also increases their satisfaction and reduces the time they have to spend returning for further treatment.

Fewer treatments, and treating the patient before the disease becomes advanced, can also save insurance companies money. Insurers are already using data mining to identify patterns that indicate fraudulent claims and bill padding by medical providers.

Sharing of medical information is limited by providers' fear of being sued, concerns about maintaining the confidentiality of patient information, and the difficultly of collecting and integrating data from widely different types of computer systems and databases. However, with the ubiquity of interactions over the internet, including

Doctors can determine the best treatment for an illness when given access to patient data.

data mining of consumer information and the publication of personal information on social media applications such as Twitter and Facebook, people, especially young people, are becoming used to the wide-scale sharing of their information, and to having less privacy. In addition, if patients begin to see a significant improvement in the quality of the health care they receive—and better outcomes for themselves, their friends, and their families—they are likely to be more willing to share their information.

Summary

Many people are concerned about the uses and potential abuses of data mining. However, there are some advantages to the practice for business, medicine, crisis intervention, and scientific exploration. It can help companies provide a better experience for their customers, as well as assist medical practitioners and social service agencies to save lives. There are a number of drawbacks to data mining as well, which will be explored in the next chapter.

FACEBOOK PRIVACY SETTINGS SHOULD BE EASY 'CAUSE CORPORATE USE OF PRIVATE INFO IS DOWNRIGHT CHEESY

Many people want to have more control over whether or not their data is captured and used.

# of Data Mining

People are concerned that their information might be used in a way that is inaccurate, unethical, or harmful to them. They are also worried about what will happen to their data if it is sold to other companies or if the firm that collected it is acquired by another company. These concerns are justified. There are a number of ways in which the personal data collected and the analysis processes can be used, accidentally or deliberately, to harm individuals. This chapter examines some of the major problems and issues related to the companies collecting and analyzing people's personal information.

Privacy

Privacy is a major issue with data mining. Data mining is, by its nature, intrusive. The data that companies collect about people is indiscriminate and wide ranging. It is often collected without the person's awareness and is sometimes sold to other companies without the person's permission. Needless to say, many people are disconcerted by the process of data mining personal information, and they object to it strenuously.

There are a number of ways that data mining can negatively affect people's privacy. Data mining relies on big data, and therefore companies constantly seek to acquire more data from ever more diverse sources. These include not only corporate databases and online retail sites, but also social networking sites. Eventually, companies can gather so much data about people from diverse sources that they know everything about them: age, gender, where they live, habits, likes, dislikes, religion, sexual preference, bank accounts, credit cards, social security numbers, and so on. It's not only creepy that strangers know this information, but sometimes it is dangerous. As previously mentioned, highly organized hackers have repeatedly broken into organizational databases and stolen information. There are other dangers as well. Employees at corporations have the ability to run queries that can produce lists of people who could be victimized in a number of ways.

Access to personal information by **malefactors** leaves people open to damage on a number of fronts. The obvious examples are identity theft and theft of money from bank accounts or credit cards. Identity theft is far and away the most common **cybercrime**. When a criminal obtains someone's personal information, he or she can open credit cards and take out loans in that person's name. The criminal can use the assumed identity to commit various types of fraud. If hackers obtain account numbers and passwords, they can steal money from accounts. Access to such information opens the door to a range of other problems. If criminals have access to someone's address, and can tell from social media posts or online purchases that he or she is going on vacation, that person can become the target of a burglary. If companies have access to information collected about a person, such as his or her religion or sexual preference, that information could affect the person when applying for a job. Demographic information about people, such as where they live and their income, can be used to target people for credit card and IRS scams. Online information that falls into the wrong hands can also affect the outcome of lawsuits.

There is no protection for privacy in the US Constitution. Most people who believe US citizens have a right to privacy refer to amendments in the Bill of Rights to support their position—for example, the Fourth Amendment, which prohibits unreasonable search and seizure, and states: "The right of the people to be secure in their persons, houses, papers, and effects, against unreasonable searches and seizures, shall not be violated." However, this rule is easier to apply to government surveillance than to the corporate collection of data. The Ninth Amendment states that even if a right is not explicitly mentioned in the Constitution, the government still cannot infringe on that right. The Fourteenth Amendment states: "No state shall make or enforce any law which shall abridge the privileges or immunities of citizens of the United States; nor shall any state deprive any person of life, liberty, or property, without due process of law; nor deny to any person within its jurisdiction the equal protection of the laws." This amendment has been interpreted by the US Supreme Court as guaranteeing the right to privacy in several cases, including the 2003 case of *Lawrence v. Texas*, which invoked the right to privacy in regard to same-sex couples.

The government is prohibited by law from compiling secret databases about American citizens, although there is some question about how well the government complies with this law. The fact is there are no laws in the United States that prohibit companies from compiling databases of information about people. There is some legislation requiring companies to give customers the right to opt out of having their data sold, and both legal and public pressure has forced companies to send annual disclosures on their policies on their use of customers' data. That is the extent of the protection afforded to consumers in the United States. That is not true of all other countries, however. More than eighty countries have adopted data-protection laws, including Canada, most countries in Europe, and many in the rest of the world. Information-privacy or data-protection laws forbid the disclosure, sale, or use of information about private individuals without their consent.

The principles of data protection under these laws include:

- There should be a stated purpose for all data collected.

- Information should not be disclosed to other organizations without the consent of the individual or due process of law.

- Individuals' information should be accurate and up to date.

- Individuals should have a means to review their data to make sure it's accurate.

- Once the purpose for the data has passed, it should be deleted.

- Transmission of personal information is only allowed to locations where equivalent personal data-protection laws exist.

- Some data is prohibited from collection because it is too sensitive, such as sexual orientation or religion.

In December 2015, the European Union drafted the General Data Protection Regulation (GDPR), which provides broad new data-protection rules. The regulation was adopted on April 27, 2016, and goes into effect on May 25, 2018. The European data-protection laws make it difficult for US companies operating in Europe to engage in the kind of data mining and selling practices common in the United States. The EU regulation targets data mining and user profiling, through provisions such as requiring individuals to "opt in"

The Data Protection Reform effort in the EU has resulted in regulations on the use of personal data.

rather than "opt out" of having their data collected, as is usual in the United States. Fines for companies that violate the regulation can be as large as 4 percent of global revenue.

Major tech firms that collect user information, such as Google and Facebook, are affected by the legislation. One provision affects "secondary uses" of personal data. A secondary use is one that is other than the purpose for which data was collected. For instance, collecting information for a legitimate purpose, such as enrollment in a rewards program, and then selling that data to other companies.

Even when US consumers agree to have their data collected, they typically consent by checking a box that authorizes a blanket privacy policy, covering all possible uses of data. In contrast, the EU regulation requires separate consent for each type of use. Thus, companies can't simply use the collected data for a different purpose without getting individuals' consent. The EU regulation also institutes tighter rules on how companies can profile or sort customers into segments according to their online data. Under this new law, people have the right to know what groups they are sorted into, why, who's using the data, and what the results of being in this group are likely to be. The regulation also requires companies to delete a person's information if requested to do so, even though this is difficult to do because the information is often contained in various databases spread across the company. Many people in the United States would like to see their privacy protected by laws like the one implemented by the EU.

At the same time that the EU is attempting to protect the privacy of its citizens, governments in Europe and the government of the United States have pressed companies such as Facebook, Google, Microsoft, Twitter, and Apple

According to a 2015 forecast by market research firm IDC, the United States will spend more money on big data and analytics than any other region in the world. It is predicted that by 2020, the US market will reach $95 billion.

for information on users, in the name of national security. So, another danger of the collection of personal data is that companies that collect it can be pressured by government law enforcement agencies to give them access to it. The requests for access to user information aren't limited to particular suspects. Rather, such requests number in the thousands, sometime tens of thousands, annually.

Data Integrity

A major issue with the collection and use of people's data is the quality of the data. Companies often combine data from different databases to create the pool of data for data mining, and there is often conflicting data in different databases. The other problem with achieving accurate data is that people's interests and needs change over time. Items and activities that interest a person at one time may not at a later time. In addition, life changes often alter people's activities and requirements. If the old data is retained too long, the profile of a person may be inaccurate. If inaccurate information is released to the public, it can create a false impression about the person.

Companies that use data mining have an insatiable need to collect ever more data. Because data mining relies on finding hidden patterns among data, there is no telling what might be important, so companies capture every piece of information they can about people. Thus, all sorts of personal information about people is retained in data warehouses. This information is accessible to both the company and hackers, and potentially to the government. Aside from the accessibility of people's data, there are two other problems associated with the indiscriminate collection of so much data: First, it becomes extremely difficult to analyze such vast quantities of data to find the data that's relevant. Second, because of the time required to analyze such large quantities of data, much of it sits in data warehouses for a long time. Therefore, by the time the data is analyzed, much of it is out of date. As a result, companies base decisions on inaccurate data, and customers are presented with information that is no longer relevant to them. The problem is made worse by the fact that companies often either fail to purge old data from their systems or have no means to do so.

Those Annoying Ads

One of the major problems with data mining is that it has become a standard tool of businesses, and therefore a vast number of companies are trying to tailor their advertising for customers by using data-mining tools. One effect of this has been a huge increase in the number and location of ads. It's practically impossible to use an electronic device without being bombarded by advertising—on game, retail,

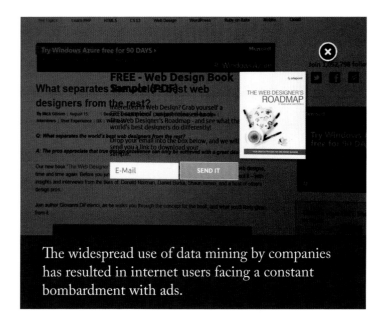

The widespread use of data mining by companies has resulted in internet users facing a constant bombardment with ads.

and educational websites; on mobile apps; on streaming services. Targeted ads now even pop up on mobile devices when a user walks by certain restaurants or stores. The constant bombardment with ads not only reduces their effectiveness but also leads consumers to do everything in their power to avoid them, from taping TV shows and skipping ads, to using ad-blocking software, to paying for ad-free versions of online media services such as Hulu.

Despite the vast amount of data collected, the data about most people is incomplete. As people become more concerned about how their personal information is being used, they are increasingly reluctant to provide detailed information about themselves in online surveys. This reluctance affects the accuracy of the assumptions companies make about them and about the groups of which they are a part. In addition, there is a great deal of inaccurate information about people in databases. People do not bother to update their information on sites they don't use often, and companies fail to purge old data from their systems. Inaccurate data affects the accuracy of the conclusions drawn from it.

Another issue is the accuracy of the assumptions made about the significance of the data. This can lead to inappropriate marketing that annoys the customer. When one is dealing with data from thousands of customers or millions of users, a small percent can mean that thousands of targeted customers are being targeted incorrectly. Even the assumptions made by systems that seek to profile individuals, such as shopping recommendation applications, are inaccurate, because they have no way of accounting for why people make purchases. Suppose your big sister is visiting with her new baby. She asks you to order some diapers online from a retailer. The data-analysis system simply assumes you are a person who needs to buy diapers and recommends other baby products. The retailer sells your data to other companies that make baby products. You may buy a set of screwdrivers, but that doesn't mean you want information on every tool available, and certainly not that you want your data sold to a company that sells pickup trucks, on the basis that someone who buys tools might be interested in buying a truck. The problem of drawing correct conclusions from data is complicated by the fact that the collection and analysis of data rely on complex data-mining algorithms. These algorithms are increasingly packaged into commercial data-mining software programs. Companies that purchase and use this software rely on it to produce accurate results, without understanding the criteria the software uses to perform its functions. If data is not accurate and it is used for corporate decision making, those decisions could turn out to be wrong.

Discrimination

The use of data mining in applications such as choosing job candidates to interview creates the potential for both deliberate and unintentional discrimination. Laws exist to protect people against discrimination on the basis of personal characteristics such as race and gender. Those laws are based

A reliance on data analysis rather than human judgment when making loan decisions can penalize minorities.

on the idea that human beings are making conscious hiring decisions, and that if they discriminate, it's deliberate. Data-mining algorithms can be created to deliberately discriminate by searching for people who possess specific characteristics, such as being white. However, data mining can also result in unintentional discrimination.

Data mining also gives companies the ability to discriminate against people on the basis of economic status. It allows companies to identify those who are well educated and affluent, and to single them out for special treatment, while ignoring those of lower socioeconomic status. When this means that the well-off get opportunities that others don't, it can increase the opportunity gap between those who are upper class and everyone else. Data mining combined with an automated computer-based risk analysis can be used to decide who gets a mortgage or loan and who doesn't. These systems rely on programmed criteria and take human judgment out of the process. The result can be discrimination against the less advantaged, and when companies rely on data mining and automated analysis systems to make decisions, it can be difficult for people to contest their rejection.

Since data mining has become a common tool in business, some companies have started using it to find job candidates and make hiring decisions. In some cases, companies search online profiles of applicants to find those whose activities mirror those of people who have made good employees in the past. One problem with this approach is that it matches candidates to the profiles of a small pool of current and past employees. If the majority of present/past employees are, for example, white males, then the search is likely to exclude female and minority candidates and produce a list of candidates who are all white men. Data mining through pattern-searching programs can also be situation-specific. If a hotel has mostly white managers, but mostly Hispanic lower-level employees, then, when searching for people to fill managerial positions, Hispanics may not appear to be a match because that characteristic is rarely found among the current successful managers. Not only is this discriminatory, but it also keeps the hotel chain from looking at the people with the most hands-on hotel experience. It has been shown repeatedly in surveys of businesses that those with more diversity tend to perform better over the long term. Therefore, looking for people who are the same is less beneficial than looking for people who are different.

This points out another key problem: the data-mining algorithm only takes into account the known characteristics of current employees in the position to be filled. Other types of people, with skills, training, and experience not possessed by people currently filling the position, may provide the company with advantages it doesn't currently possess. This is particularly true at a time when societal values, generational preferences, and technology on all levels are changing rapidly. People with new skills and insights may be needed for the company to remain competitive. In short, as the old ways of doing things are continually replaced by new ones, people with new skills and knowledge are required, and these people, by definition, are not in the employee pool that candidates are being compared to. A case in point: Prior to the terrorist attacks of 9/11, CIA analysts were primarily people who had been hired with the idea that the Soviet Union was America's greatest threat. There was a dearth of surveillance personnel who spoke Arabic and had expertise on the Middle East. This changed after the attacks of 9/11, when the agency's emphasis shifted. However, if it had been using **pattern matching** based on the old employees to hire new employees, it would have been hiring people with the wrong skills and knowledge. The same applies to corporations. A company focused on making software products that run on PCs would have been left behind when the online world shifted to mobile devices if it simply searched for new employees who had the same skill sets as its existing employees.

Misuse of Data

Another negative of data mining is the misuse of customer data by companies. When a company combines a person's personal information with very large data sets that contain other information, it can discover facts that are likely to be true about people, such as their sexual preference or the fact that they suffer from a disease. Once this information is revealed, it is accessible—to the company that discovered it, to other companies they may sell the information to, and to employees or outsiders who might be able to access the data. People like to have control over what information they release about themselves to other people and the world at large. This ability to discover and release information about them—or use it against them—makes many people uncomfortable.

Then there is the issue of what a company will or should do if it discovers information that is of importance to people. What if data-mining results reveal that a customer is likely to have a serious disease such as Parkinson's disease, Alzheimer's disease, diabetes, or clinical depression? Is the company ethically obligated to inform the customer of the

Data mining can be misused by lenders to target people who will not be able to pay off a loan, resulting in higher interest payments.

possibility that he or she has an illness that might require medical treatment? Companies might be reluctant to do so because customers often become upset when they find out that companies have that level of information about them. If this fact became widely known, the pubic might demand regulations like those passed in the EU to restrict the data-mining efforts of companies. Target has gone so

The Sony Pictures Hack

One threat to data stored in company systems is hackers. Often company systems lack adequate security to protect their data from sophisticated hackers. The Sony Pictures hack is one example of such system vulnerability.

On November 24, 2014, hackers broke into the Sony Pictures computer systems and released, on the internet, confidential data including personal information about Sony Pictures employees and their families, salaries, and other facts. In December, a group called The Guardians of Peace demanded that Sony cancel the release of its film *The Interview*, a comedy revolving around a plot to assassinate North Korean leader Kim Jong-Eun. The group threatened terrorist attacks at cinemas that showed the film, and Sony chose to release the film digitally instead. US intelligence officials blamed North Korea for the cyberattack as well as the threats. North Korea denied responsibility.

Some of the employees whose data was stolen were subsequently the victims of identity theft. In October 2015, Sony agreed to pay affected current and former employees as much as $4.5 million in a settlement, with lawyers getting another $3.5 million. The agreement included $2 million to reimburse employees who paid for their own identity theft protection measures, and up to $2.5 million for employees who were victims of identity theft.

Former employees alleged the company was aware that it did not have adequate measures in place to protect its data.

The Sony Pictures hack allowed criminals to intimidate cinemas into not showing the film *The Interview*.

They also claimed Sony had experienced two breaches before the 2014 attack. These ex-employees claimed Sony had made a decision that it would be less expensive to accept the risk of a hack than to fix the security issues. In this case, it was employees who suffered as a result of a company's insufficient data protection. However, it could just as easily have been members of the public whose personal data is stored in a company's database systems.

A person working for a company can obtain and misuse customers' data for personal enrichment.

far as to disguise what it knows by emailing ads suitable for pregnant women along with offers for non-pregnancy-oriented products, to hide the fact they know a customer is pregnant. If the company finds out that a customer is likely to have a serious disease and doesn't warn him or her, is the company ethically or legally culpable? This is one way in which the collection and analysis of personal data by companies is raising new regulatory and legal issues.

One type of misuse of information has been occurring since before data mining became commonplace. Banks, credit card companies, and mortgage lenders make money from interest paid on loans and the fees they collect when borrowers go over their credit limit or are late with their payments. Therefore, these lenders have an incentive to identify potential borrowers who will not be able to pay off their credit cards or loans, but will keep making minimum payments each month. Data mining makes it easier for financial companies to learn which people would be good targets for ads for credit cards and loans—not because they are good credit risks but because they are poor ones. These types of predatory practices contributed significantly to the financial meltdown in 2008. This is a risky practice that is not likely to be good for the economy as a whole, and certainly not for the people who are encouraged to take out loans they will have trouble repaying. Other companies could take a similar approach to sell high-ticket products.

An extensive collection of user data stored by a company makes an attractive target for hackers. External hackers aren't the only danger to large repositories of customer data. The existence of databases full of customer data can present a temptation to employees of companies as well. According to a 2016 article in *Information Age*:

As part of its 2016 Data Breach Report, Verizon analyzed more than 100,000 security incidents from countries around the world. Of these, there were more than 10,000 insider incidents, including 172 with confirmed data disclosure.

Among those affected were AT&T, Target, and Home Depot. Insider abuse of customer data can be either **negligent** or **malicious**. In negligent misuse, an employee accidentally releases information. Although the results can be problematic or embarrassing, there is no intent to misuse the information. A more dangerous type of insider data breach is done with malicious intent. In this case, an employee accesses the database deliberately to steal user information such as account or social security numbers. There are two major reasons employees steal data: anger and gain. Disgruntled employees might steal data in order to get back at an employer they feel has treated them unfairly. Other employees may simply steal data to sell. Malicious misuse is much more common than negligent misuse. Verizon's study found that out of 230 insider data breach incidents that took place in 2015, more than 60 percent were malicious in nature. The online black market for data provides a financial incentive that is too much for some employees to resist, so they steal and sell information. Cyber espionage is also becoming more common. In cyber espionage, employees are paid by other companies or governments to steal confidential data.

Contrary to what one might expect, most of the employees who engaged in data theft were not high-ranking information technology experts but ordinary end users who had access to data as part of their job. This fact is worrying for customers whose information is stored in databases in companies across the country and sometimes the world. For example, in 2014, AT&T employees at international call centers were found to have sold information on US customers, including social security numbers, to third parties. A small number of breaches are the result of collusion between someone at the company and an outside agent. However, 80 percent of these acts were committed by someone in the company acting alone.

The inside data thief isn't always an employee of the company. Sometimes the theft is committed by an employee of a supplier, service, or partner organization that is given access to the computer system through a remote connection. Many large corporations allow suppliers direct access so they can automatically fill inventory. Access is also often granted to service organizations, such as those that supply paycheck-processing or employee-benefit services, and to dealers or companies working jointly on projects. Therefore, there may be a large number of people only peripherally associated with the company who have the opportunity to carry out an insider attack.

Fast Fact

According to information services company Deltek, information security policies and management programs in the federal government will result in federal agencies increasing their spending on cloud computing and big data services from $2.4 billion in 2015 to $6.2 billion by 2020.

One reason that companies' data is so vulnerable to insider attacks is that, in most companies, computer security is focused on keeping external hackers from gaining access to the system, not company employees. Unless companies have implemented a system that tracks employee access to the company's data stores, it is difficult to identify insiders who are misusing data. Also, it generally takes much longer to catch an internal data thief, often months and sometimes years, than it does an outside thief.

Big Brother *Is* Watching You

Data mining and target advertising have reached the point where many businesses are tracking people in real time through their applications. It can become both distracting and disconcerting to have applications tracking your every move, popping up restaurant menus and offers from stores near you and offering unsolicited advice on sightseeing destinations in your vicinity. It's one thing for a merchant to keep track of your past purchases, it's another to have a company, or in some cases multiple companies, monitoring everything you do.

Businesses are not the only organizations interested in your activities. The government and law enforcement have an avid interest in the data collected by businesses. When a terrorist attack occurs, the government often attempts to extend its reach into personal information held at social media, telephone, and other companies. Government agencies seek constantly to extend their control over data and to gain ever-increasing access to data collected by companies. The problem is that if companies give in to these agencies' pressure at times of national crisis, it is likely that such access

Companies can track people via the applications on their phone, sending unsolicited information and offers.

will become the norm. Little by little, the use of citizens' data by the government will increase, whittling away at the protections granted by the Constitution.

Law enforcement would also like to get access to all that data. Data mining that is capable of deducing that a person is pregnant or has a disease can also be used to create a picture of someone who is likely to be engaged in illegal activity. Earlier we asked what a company should do if it finds that a person is ill. Another question is what a company should do if it finds that a person might be engaged in illegal activity. What if the activity is not terrorism, but a run-of-the-mill crime—a crime that has not yet been committed and that a person may or may not commit? Routine monitoring of citizens for suspicious activity is forbidden by the Fourth Amendment. If the government or federal or local law enforcement agencies take advantage of information uncovered by companies routinely analyzing data, they are violating the protections afforded by the Constitution. Even if they were not, there are problems with such searches. People who appear to be engaging in suspicious activity may not be planning to do anything wrong. A person may be planning to do something wrong and then decide not to. Even worse, a person might be a false positive—someone who appears to fit the profile but is entirely innocent. Being under this type of surveillance limits the freedom of people. It makes people worry about how everything they do might be interpreted. Being wrongly accused can ruin people's lives, and even being correctly accused violates constitutional measures designed to protect people's freedom and allow them to live without fear of government intervention in their lives. In the worst case, the government or other organizations could use the data they access to single out specific groups for mistreatment. This is why protections against arbitrary searches of people's records were written into the Bill of Rights attached to the Constitution to begin with.

All the negative effects of company data mining recounted in this chapter illustrate the need for better security and for adequate protections against inappropriate and unauthorized collection and use of people's data.

Data center professionals are working on ever more sophisticated ways of collecting and analyzing data.

Future Holds

This is unquestionably the age of big data. We are likely to see continued growth in the acquisition of data and the application of data mining to find uses for it. Some future trends are explored here.

Advances in Technology

Two opposing technological forces are fighting it out on the landscape of data mining and advertising: On one hand, companies are developing new ways of monitoring people's behavior and collecting information about them. On the other, companies are working on ways to block the insistent ads that other companies inundate people with.

Mobile advertising has been one of the fastest-growing areas of advertising in the 2000s. However, application developers are creating tools that will allow users to block ads on their mobile devices in much the same way that pop-up blockers block ads on desktop PCs. Apple has gone as far as to incorporate an ad blocker into recent iterations of its software.

In their insatiable need for data, companies are trying to find new ways to gather information about consumers. Samsung has already tried inserting technology into its smart TVs that logs watchers' viewing activities and voice commands. Initially, when people objected, the company pointed out that the terms of the user agreement stated that users' spoken words "could be captured and transmitted to a third party." Bad publicity in the media and customer outrage eventually made Samsung tell people how to switch off the feature. However, once one company discovers how to do something, others often pick up on the concept. Who knows what devices in the future will capture user behavior and conversations in real time?

The Samsung Smart TV has the capability to watch users while users watch it.

Microsoft and Salesforce.com are working on applications that would allow users with no programming skills to analyze data. This type of tool would allow people with neither programming nor database application experience to find information they are looking for in databases. Microsoft and Salesforce are not alone. The growth in the number of companies implementing data mining and the growing size of the projects will lead to a shortage of skilled workers. A lack of qualified staff is likely to fuel the creation of easy-to-use tools that can be applied by less experienced—even untrained—employees. The initial purpose of such tools may be to allow workers at companies to search their own databases, but it's only a matter of time until malefactors find ways to apply this software for their own purposes. Such access would open the door to all types of uses and abuses, from sending spam and engaging in unwanted telemarketing to blackmail and burglary. Granted, there are already crooks engaging in this activity, but there would likely be many more of them if it could be done without understanding how to code or how to access the data. This would make it even easier for insiders to obtain valuable information from company databases.

Fast Data

The latest trend in data processing is "fast data." The concept of fast data is to speed up the processing of big data so that it is more timely and thus more useful for decision making. Companies are working on ways to analyze data as it is collected and stream the results in real time. In a process called "stream processing," inbound data is analyzed as it is being collected, and conclusions are continuously updated. This process avoids some of the problems of using out-of-

Fast-data technology helps companies automatically distribute orders to specific warehouses so there are no delays in getting products to customers.

date data, but it exacerbates the problem of making decisions based on incomplete or inaccurate data. It is also likely to make conclusions about individuals less accurate, if it looks at, for example, their most recent purchases, as opposed to their purchases over time.

There are some legitimate uses for fast-data technology. The most obvious one is fraud detection, because this process makes it possible to detect a possibly fraudulent purchase faster—and even if the transaction turns out to be legitimate, no harm is done by calling the customer and checking. It also has an application in real-time order routing, in which a company receives continuous information on how many units are being filled at each location, so that orders can be filled at less busy locations, smoothing out the loads so that transportation vehicles are filled consistently and reducing bottlenecks.

On the other hand, the technology lends itself to mass surveillance, allowing the processing of data showing people's activities and movements in real time, a process that is open to abuse by government and law enforcement agencies. If information about a person's activities is streamed and processed as these activities occur, any behavior deemed undesirable could potentially be flagged in the same way that fraudulent purchases are, and individuals could be singled out for punitive action by a company or the government.

Companies are investigating ways of using **machine learning** to create data-analysis systems that can learn from previous conclusions and can then create their own new analytical algorithms without human intervention. Machine learning is a process that combines artificial intelligence software with large data sets. Machine learning programs examine large data sets, using a set of initial assumptions, and then, depending on what the data shows, the programs adjust those assumptions and create new algorithms.

Such programs can provide companies with information on hidden relationships, but they have serious problems. First, when companies rely on computers to make decisions for them, the computers all tend to come to the same conclusions, which leads companies to create the same products, cater to the same customers, or make the same financial decisions. This reduces the availability of other products and services. It also increases the amount of discrimination against people who are not the most affluent or desirable customers. Such programs encourage all the companies in a given industry to make the same decisions at the same time; this means that many things people want or need become unavailable to those who are not in the majority. It also means that companies wind up competing for the same group of customers, and only some companies can win because there is a finite number of those customers. The companies that don't do as well either fail or downsize, which adversely affects the economy.

Second, one of the latest approaches to data mining suggests that fast data and "actionable data" are more important than big data. The argument goes: Companies only use a fraction of the data they collect anyway. Grabbing a chunk of data coming in via fast-data streaming, analyzing that data, and acting on the results is more effective for getting decisions made than attempting to analyze a large amount of data that has been collected. Of course, there's no guarantee that the data that is being analyzed in this sampling process is accurate or representative of the population being studied. The dangers of making judgments on the basis of a small sample of data were adequately demonstrated in 2016, when the vast majority of pollsters were wrong about whether Britain would leave the European Union, and were wrong again a short while later about whether Donald Trump or Hillary Clinton would win the US presidential election. There is such a thing as making decisions too fast and doing inadequate analysis.

Third, because the algorithms used to analyze data will be created by the system itself, it is difficult to establish whether they will be finding the best solutions or taking into account all—or even the most important—elements. It will be difficult, if not impossible, to tell people why a financial decision or hiring decision was made about them because

Predictions about the 2016 election for president were wrong because pollsters used only a sample of the data.

the algorithms aren't based on assumptions made by people at the company. All that can be said is that, according to the computer criteria, a person doesn't qualify. If this argument is carried to the absurd extreme, the result of continuous refinement of risk-management financial programs would logically be that only rich people should be given loans, since they are the only people guaranteed to repay them, and the only people who would be considered good job candidates are those who are exactly like those who are already employed by the company and performing well.

Companies are aware of some of the problems with relying on machine learning. In response, they're looking into an even more advanced approach to artificial intelligence, called "**cognitive computing.**" Cognitive computing uses self-learning systems, data mining, pattern recognition, and natural language processing (the ability to recognize concepts represented by words) to create a simulation of the way the human brain processes information. One problem with these systems is that they can be too accurate. In 2016, Facebook tried to create a chatbot, a software application that would chat with users as if it were a person. The problem was that it issued so many offensive slurs and used such offensive language, based on what it had learned in its exploration of conversations, that it had to be removed. Clearly, mimicking human beings without societal controls (such as censure and the threat of punishment) and emotional controls (such as guilt and fear of embarrassment) that keep human beings in line is fraught with pitfalls. Certainly such a system is not going to worry about whether people of lower socioeconomic status are being discriminated against.

Monetizing Big Data

The systems, software, and staff required to collect and analyze data are very expensive. Companies are constantly looking for ways to control their costs. One obvious way to defray the cost of data mining is to sell the data to other companies, either those in related industries or those that lack the capacity to gather and analyze big data on their own. In addition, smaller companies that possess databases of information will take advantage of the market for data by selling their data to companies doing big data analysis. Further, companies will arise whose sole purpose is to collect and sell data to companies engaged in big data analysis. This type of company is analogous to the companies that once collected names and addresses and sold mailing lists to other companies or organizations for marketing or donation-solicitation purposes. To go along with their data purchases, companies will be able to buy off-the-shelf and custom data-analysis algorithms. There are already some companies that offer such algorithms for sale, and the number is likely to grow.

Data Sharing Between Business and Government

The car service Uber has developed a tool it calls "God View" for tracking customers in real time. This tool shows customers waiting for cars in silhouette, supposedly to protect their identity. However, since it doesn't disguise location information, it's still possible to figure out who people are. According to an article in *Forbes* magazine, the technology has already been misused for entertainment at Uber parties. It's easy to see how technology of this

Surveillance technology could be used by law enforcement or the government to track people's activities, even if they haven't yet committed a crime.

sort could be developed for use in tracking people for surveillance purposes.

In the future, governments or cash-strapped agencies will be tempted to **monetize** the valuable data resources they have collected, especially as the costs of data warehousing and maintenance mount. They will find personal data to be of interest and value to companies.

Research organizations have a great interest in accessing data held by the government, businesses, and nonprofits. Sometimes organizations that make data available to researchers use a process called "pseudo-anonymization," which removes names from records in a database and replaces them with an identification number. This supposedly provides anonymity for the records. The problem is that software exists that can use the identification number and other data contained in the files to reverse the anonymization relatively easily, allowing access to confidential information.

The Ethical Use of Data

As the use of big data continues to grow, there will likely be more agitation on the part of privacy advocates and the public to better control the collection of people's data. Trust and Predictive Technologies 2016 is a survey that was conducted by the public relations firm Edelman and the University of Cambridge Psychometrics Research Centre. The study surveyed more than thirty-four thousand people around the world on the subject of predictive technologies, which include data mining, machine learning, and related technologies used to collect and analyze people's personal data. Among the study's findings (see http://www.slideshare.net/ EdelmanInsights/trust-predictive-technologies-2016) were: 71 percent of people believed that companies with access to their personal data were using it unethically; 26 percent of people trusted the government not to sell their data; people were more accepting of the use of data mining for improving the quality of life than for commercial purposes; 84 percent of people surveyed supported the idea of using data mining to improve health care, whereas only 47 percent felt it should be used to set the price of their car insurance; people were open to the idea of using predictive analytic technology to help them make the best financial decisions, but the majority were against the use of this type of technology by banks to make decisions on who should be given a mortgage (62 percent) or a person's likelihood of defaulting on a loan (67 percent).

These attitudes represent a realistic assessment of many of the dangers of data mining discussed in this book.

Businesses will not turn back the clock on data mining. In the University of Cambridge study, 77 percent of marketing and communications professionals felt their organization should invest in predictive data technology, and 94 percent felt that data mining was important to understanding the psychological characteristics of customers. Businesses are going to go on expanding their collection and use of people's data. There will likely be continued issues with the deliberate and accidental misuse of data. The hope is that the financial liability associated with allowing inside and external data hacks, as well as the bad publicity associated with these data breaches, will force companies to improve the security of their systems. Certainly, better internal and external controls are required to make sure that data is being collected and used in accordance with companies' policies.

One of the conclusions of the University of Cambridge study was that the ethical use of people's data has to be a key part of businesses' use of data mining. However, Edelman's measure of public trust, the Trust Barometer, shows that in 2016, less than 50 percent of people in twenty-eight countries surveyed trusted businesses and government. In addition, market research firm Gartner Inc. predicts that 50 percent of business ethics violations will relate to data by 2018. Public embarrassment and pressure from customers, as well as the fear that people will insist on regulation if data is not better controlled, are the best means currently available to force companies to improve their policies, procedures, and security. Indeed, some experts feel that public pressure will force companies to pay more attention to their policies on protecting privacy. However, in the University of Cambridge study, 78 percent of people surveyed felt that the threat of negative media coverage would not be sufficient to stop businesses from misusing people's data. Therefore, there is great support for some type of regulation and enforcement to protect people from the misuse of their data. However, in the United States, it is unlikely that there will be regulation of the collection and use of people's data any time soon, given that, as of 2017, the country has a president and Congress that are exceedingly pro-business and anti-regulation.

November 30, 1936 British mathematician Alan Turing publishes a paper, "On Computable Numbers," in which he introduces the idea of a universal machine that can be programmed to perform computations. The concepts in his paper form the basis for the development of computers.

Mid-1940 Alan Turing develops a machine that deciphers the encrypted Enigma code used by Nazi Germany to send military messages. Germany changes the cipher it uses on its Enigma machine daily, but Turing's machine is able to read the messages despite the changes. The information culled from the intercepted messages is credited with shortening World War II by several years.

1943 Warren McCulloch and Walter Pitts create the first conceptual model of a neural network and describe it in a paper, "A Logical Calculus of the Ideas Immanent in Nervous Activity." A neural network is a form of artificial intelligence modeled on the way neurons work in the human brain.

September 1965 Lawrence J. Fogel forms Decision Science, Inc., the first company to apply a form of artificial intelligence called "evolutionary programming" to real-world problems. Evolutionary programming uses a process modeled on natural evolution to arrive at solutions to problems.

1970s The development of sophisticated database management systems and data warehouses makes it possible to store and query huge quantities of data.

January 1, 1974 Peter Naur publishes *Concise Survey of Computer Methods* in Sweden and the United States. He defines "data science" as "The science of dealing with data, once they have been established, while the relation of the data to what they represent is delegated to other fields and sciences."

1975 John Henry Holland publishes *Adaptation in Natural and Artificial Systems*, in which he describes a form of artificial intelligence called "genetic algorithms." Genetic algorithms behave like genes that are continuously modified as they process data.

1977 The International Statistical Institute creates a new division: the International Association for Statistical Computing (IASC). IASC's mission is "to link traditional statistical methodology, modern computer technology, and the knowledge of domain experts in order to convert data into information and knowledge."

1989 Gregory Piatetsky-Shapiro coins the phrase "Knowledge Discovery in Databases" (KDD) for the first workshop on the subject, and this term becomes popular in the artificial intelligence community to describe early data mining.

1990s Retail companies and the financial community start using data mining to predict trends. Work begins in cognitive computing, an advanced form of artificial intelligence, incorporating data mining, pattern recognition, and natural language processes to mimic human thought processes. The term "big data" appears in the late 1990s.

April 2001 William S. Cleveland publishes "Data Science: An Action Plan for Expanding the Technical Areas of the Field of Statistics," a plan to expand the field of statistics, through the incorporation of computing, into a "data science."

June 17, 2003 The book *Moneyball*, by Michael Lewis, shows how the Oakland Athletics used a statistical, data-driven approach to select players based on specific qualities and on value, and assembled a team that reached the 2002 and 2003 playoffs. The book changes the way many sports teams approach assembling their teams.

February 18, 2015 D. J. Patil is appointed the first Chief Data Scientist at the White House.

December 15, 2015 The European Union enacts the European Union General Data Protection Regulation (GDPR), which institutes broad new data-protection rules.

algorithm A series of rules that gets translated into computer code that tells the computer how to solve a problem.

anomaly Something that is abnormal; an incident that doesn't fit a pattern.

artificial intelligence The ability of a computer to perform operations that include learning and decision making.

atypical Not normal or usual; out of the ordinary.

client/server computer system A type of computer network that consists of a powerful computer called a server that stores data and programs, and a series of desktop computers that are connected to it.

cloud A collection of remote computers that are run by a service company, contain data and programs belonging to companies, and are accessed by those companies over the internet.

cognitive computing A form of artificial intelligence that combines data mining, pattern recognition, and natural language processing to mimic human thought processes.

consolidate To combine into a coherent whole.

correlation A relationship or connection between two or more things.

cybercrime Crime that takes place on a computer system or over the internet.

database A collection or set of data housed on a computer system that can be accessed in different ways.

data warehouse A large store of information gathered from various sources.

domain expert A person who is an expert in a particular field, such as medicine or finance.

heyday The period of greatest strength or success.

hypothesis A proposed explanation based on incomplete information that forms a starting point for further investigation.

integrate To combine two or more parts to produce a whole.

knowledge base A store of information gathered from domain experts in a particular field, such as medicine, and stored on a computer system.

machine learning A type of artificial intelligence in which a computer alters its programming in response to the data it encounters.

malefactor A criminal or an evildoer; someone doing something with an evil intent.

malicious Intending or intended to do harm.

millennial A person who reached young adulthood around 2000.

monetize To make or generate money from.

natural language Ordinary written or spoken language.

negligent Not taking the proper care or precautions.

pattern matching A computer process that finds data that fits into a pattern exactly.

payday lender A company that lends money for a short period, for example until a person gets his or her paycheck.

point-of-sale system A computerized cash register system, which records sales information.

promotion A special offer designed to get a customer to buy a product or service.

retention In business, keeping a customer.

scattershot Spread all over randomly, like pellets shot from a gun.

statistician A mathematician who specializes in calculating probabilities and trends.

Sumerian Coming from an ancient region in southern Mesopotamia (now Iraq), which was initially settled sometime between 5500 and 4000 BCE.

transaction A sale or other exchange, now usually carried out on a computer.

Books

Brown, Meta S. *Data Mining for Dummies*. Hoboken, NJ: John Wiley, 2014.

Lewis, Michael. *Moneyball: The Art of Winning an Unfair Game*. New York: W. W. Norton, 2004.

Mayer-Schönberger, Viktor, and Kenneth Cukier. *Big Data: A Revolution That Will Transform How We Live, Work, and Think*. London, UK: John Murray, 2014.

Payton, Theresa, and Ted Claypool. *Privacy in the Age of Big Data: Recognizing Threats, Defending Your Rights, and Protecting Your Family*. Lanham, MD: Rowman & Littlefield, 2015.

Online Articles

Atlantic

"Welcome to Smarter Basketball"

http://www.theatlantic.com/entertainment/archive/2015/06/nba-data-analytics/396776

This story explains the way analytics is changing how basketball players are scouted and valued.

Electronic Frontier Foundation

"Privacy"

https://www.eff.org/issues/privacy

This website contains links to stories on many of the issues surrounding privacy.

Predictive Analytics Today

"What Is Predictive Analytics?"

http://www.predictiveanalyticstoday.com/what-is-predictive-analytics

Using text and graphics, this article explains all aspects of predictive analytics.

SAS

"Big Data: What It Is and Why It Matters"

http://www.sas.com/en_us/insights/big-data/what-is-big-data.html

A major analytics company explains what companies can do with the large amounts of information they gather.

Videos

The Great Courses

"Big Data: How Data Analytics Is Changing the World"

http://www.thegreatcourses.com/courses/big-data-how-data-analytics-is-transforming-the-world.html

This DVD set explains the concepts and accomplishments of data analytics.

The Great Courses

"The Surveillance State: Big Data, Freedom, and You"

http://www.thegreatcourses.com/courses/the-surveillance-state-big-data-freedom-and-you.html

This DVD set discusses the questions about privacy, security, civil liberties, and more, raised by the usage of data mining and big data.

Public Broadcasting Service

"The Human Face of Big Data"

http://www.pbs.org/show/human-face-big-data

With the rapid emergence of digital devices, this video series explores "the invisible force that is changing human lives in ways from the microscopic to the gargantuan." Also available on DVD and from Amazon Video.

Books

Scheer, Robert. *They Know Everything About You: How Data-Collecting Corporations and Snooping Government Agencies Are Destroying Democracy.* New York: Nation Books, 2015.

Schneier, Bruce. *Data and Goliath: The Hidden Battles to Collect Your Data and Control Your World.* New York: W. W. Norton, 2015.

Online Articles

Borocas, Solon. "Losing Out on Employment Because of Big Data Mining." *New York Times*, August 8, 2014. http://www.nytimes.com/roomfordebate/2014/08/06/is-big-data-spreading-inequality/losing-out-on-employment-because-of-big-data-mining.

CNBC/Reuters. "Yahoo Says New Hack Affected 1 Billion Users, Separate from Earlier Attack." CNBC, December 14, 2016. http://www.cnbc.com/2016/12/14/yahoo-says-new-hack-affected-1-billion-users-separate-from-earlier-attack.html.

Dwoskin, Elizabeth. "EU Data-Privacy Law Raises Daunting Prospects for US Companies." *Wall Street Journal*, December 16, 2015. http://www.wsj.com/

articles/eu-data-privacy-law-raises-daunting-prospects-for-u-s-companies-1450306033.

Fiegerman, Seth. "Yahoo Says 500 Million Accounts Stolen." CNN, September 23, 2016. http://money.cnn.com/2016/09/22/technology/yahoo-data-breach.

Furnas, Alexander. "Everything You Want to Know About Data Mining, but Were Afraid to Ask." *Atlantic*, April 3, 2012. http://www.theatlantic.com/technology/archive/2012/04/everything-you-wanted-to-know-about-data-mining-but-were-afraid-to-ask/255388.

Guerena, Elisia. "Crisis Text Line Uses SMS Data Mining to Save Lives." MobileCommons, October 13, 2014. https://www.mobilecommons.com/blog/2014/10/sms-data-mining-saves-lives.

Gupta, Vin. "Without Good Analysis Big Data Is Just a Big Trash Dump." *Entrepreneur*, May 21, 2015. https://www.entrepreneur.com/article/246470.

"How Alan Turing Cracked the Enigma Code." Imperial War Museums. Accessed March 13, 2017. http://www.iwm.org.uk/history/how-alan-turing-cracked-the-enigma-code

Kadlec, Dan. "Privacy? Here's How Data Mining Might Actually Help Consumers." *Time*, March 6, 2012. http://business.time.com/2012/03/06/privacy-heres-how-data-mining-might-actually-help-consumers.

Kaufman, Roy. "How Traders Are Using Text and Data Mining to Beat the Market." *Street*, February 12, 2015. https://www.thestreet.com/story/13044694/2/how-traders-are-using-text-and-data-mining-to-beat-the-market.html.

Li, Ray. "The History of Data Mining." Dataconomy, June 16, 2016. http://dataconomy.com/2016/06/history-data-mining/

Marr, Bernard. "Big Data: 20 Mind-Boggling Facts Everyone Must Read." *Forbes*, September 30, 2015. http://www.forbes.com/sites/bernardmarr/2015/09/30/big-data-20-mind-boggling-facts-everyone-must-read/#2d3918556c1d.

———. "17 Predictions about the Future of Big Data Everyone Should Read." *Forbes*, March 15, 2016. http://www.forbes.com/sites/bernardmarr/2016/03/15/17-predictions-about-the-future-of-big-data-everyone-should-read/#6aabf2dd157c.

McFarland, Matt. "The Incredible Potential and Dangers of Data Mining Health Records." *Washington Post*, October 14, 2014. https://www.washingtonpost.com/news/innovations/wp/2014/10/01/the-incredible-potential-and-dangers-of-data-mining-health-records/?utm_term=.03a5680b2d83.

Mullens, Robert. "Raspberry Pi Touring Machines." University of Cambridge Computer Laboratory. Accessed March 13, 2017. https://www.cl.cam.ac.uk/projects/raspberrypi/tutorials/turing-machine/one.html

Oracle Corporation. "Data Mining Concepts." Oracle Help Center. Retrieved December 7, 2016. https://docs.oracle.com/cd/B28359_01/datamine.111/b28129/process.htm#DMCON002.

Pasierbinska-Wilson, Zuzanna. "When Data Collection Goes Wrong: 10 Examples of Identity Data Being Misused." *Target Marketing*, January 13, 2016. http://www.targetmarketingmag.com/article/when-data-collection-goes-wrong-10-examples-identity-data-being-misused/all.

Pettersson, Edvard. "Sony to Pay as Much as $8 Million to Settle Data-Breach Case." *Bloomberg Technology*, October 20, 2015. https://www.bloomberg.com/news/

articles/2015-10-20/sony-to-pay-as-much-as-8-million-to-settle-data-breach-claims.

Press, Gil. "A Very Short History of Data Science." *Forbes*, May 28, 2013. http://www.forbes.com/sites/gilpress/2013/05/28/a-very-short-history-of-data-science/#39b9864469fd.

Rossi, Ben. "How Common Is Insider Misuse—and How Can It Be Neutralized?" *Information Age*, September 20, 2016. http://www.information-age.com/common-insider-misuse-123462235.

Ryan, Tom. "Family Dollar Tests Basket Analysis." *RetailWire*, March 11, 2010. http://www.retailwire.com/discussion/family-dollar-tests-basket-analysis.

Stanley, Jay. "Eight Problems with 'Big Data.'" American Civil Liberties Union, April 25, 2012. https://www.aclu.org/blog/eight-problems-big-data.

Stein, Joel. "Data Mining: How Companies Now Know Everything About You." *Time*, March 10, 2011. http://content.time.com/time/magazine/article/0,9171,2058205,00.html.

University of Cambridge Psychometrics Research Centre, Edelman. "Trust and Predictive Technologies 2016." SlideShare. Retrieved February 28, 2017. http://www. slideshare.net/EdelmanInsights/trust-predictive-technologies-2016.

Zhuo, TX. "'Big Data' Is No Longer Enough. It's Now All About 'Fast Data.'" *Entrepreneur*, May 13, 2016. https://www.entrepreneur.com/article/273561.

Index

Jeri Freedman has a BA from Harvard University. She worked in high-technology companies for fifteen years. She is the author of numerous nonfiction books, including *America Debates: Civil Liberties and Terrorism, America Debates: Privacy vs. Security, In the News: The US Economic Crisis, and Robots Through History.*